Pleasing the Diners

Translations from the Latin of Martial

R. L. Barth

To Susan, Ann, Eric, and Trig

If Martial is minor then we had better redefine major

—Turner Cassity

Contubernales Books
www.contubernalesbooks.com

First published 2026
Printed in the United States of America

*For their encouragement and material assistance,
I would like to thank A. M. Juster and Patrick Kurp.
I would also like to thank Suzanne Doyle, Gerald Wandio,
and, of course, my wife, Susan, for additional encouragement.*

*Some of these poems appeared in Anecdotal Evidence, Blue Unicorn,
Chicago Review, Classical Outlook, Cresset, Earthenware (Havertown, PA:
Drastic Measures, 1988), Epigrams of Martial Englished by Divers Hands
(Berkeley, CA: University of California Press, 1987), Plains Poetry Journal,
and Poetry Made Easy (Lanham, MD: University Press of America, 2002).*

A Note on These Translations

I returned from my thirteen-month Vietnam tour of duty in March 1969. With fewer than ninety days remaining on my three-year enlistment, I was granted an Honorable Discharge from the United States Marine Corps. I had enlisted after graduating from high school, wanting nothing to do with college. In 1969, however, feeling at loose ends and having the GI Bill, I decided to give college a try. I was fortunate: in my early semesters, I had a couple of excellent English professors who set my academic course. During those early semesters, I decided I also wanted to write poetry. Like most young writers, I had neither a style nor a subject matter.

My epiphany, if you will, came in my third year when I took a class in Literary Criticism from Prof. Tom Zaniello. One of the assigned texts was Yvor Winters's *In Defense of Reason.* Winters made perfect sense to me, and I began to explore his writings and the writing of the poets associated with him. Most important for me, I discovered his revolutionary essay on the sixteenth-century English plain-style poets. I read all of them—George Gascoigne, Barnabe Googe, George Turbervile, Lord Vaux and many others—including the period epigrammatists. I remember reading Timothy Kendall's *Flovvers of Epigrammes.* Kendall is neither a first-rate poet nor a first-rate translator, but his book contained various translations of Martial's epigrams. That was my introduction to Martial. I knew I had found a smart aleck brother, and I read his work voraciously in translation. It would take me many years to perfect my own plain style and some years before I returned to my love and practice of epigrams. It was then, some forty-five years ago, that I began to translate Martial. At one point in the late 1980's I had a typescript of some two hundred translations. I'll skip the story and simply say that I lost that typescript. (This was before the age of computers.) That was disheartening, of course, and I left off translating for some years. But return I did. Martial just meant too much to me, as he still does, to abandon him. Thus, I arrive at this book.

I think it would be too grandiose to say that I have a "theory of translation," but I do have my methods and perhaps a paragraph or two discussing them would not be amiss. If there is a Platonic Ideal of a verse translation of Martial, it would be an excellent poem in English that would also serve as a literal translation of the original, at least making some necessary allowance for Latin word order. This translation would embody the rhetoric, tropes, connotations, allusions, and feelings of the original precisely. Obviously, that Platonic Ideal is impossible to achieve. Translators must make choices, and I will try to make mine clear.

Let me say a few words about the epigrams I have translated. The core of this book lies in the poems I translated because I admire them deeply. Early on, those poems would have been the smart-alecky satiric poems about the hypocrisies and foibles Martial observed in Roman society. In recent years, however, I find myself more attracted to and admiring of epigrams that wouldn't be perceived as "typical" Martial epigrams. Two examples would be the epigram to Marcellinus (IX.45) and ones devoted to Roman history like that on the revolt of Saturninus (IV.11). (Of course, I have to find the original amenable to my abilities. Much as I admire Martial's epigram on little Erotion, I have tried to translate it off and on for more than thirty years, and I've never been able to achieve what I consider a satisfactory version.)

This book has many epigrams that aren't among those I admire deeply, although I certainly like most of them well enough. In fact, I would go so far as to dispute Martial's comment on how a book was made: "Some good, some bad, some so-so odds and ends" (I.16). I'd say he's covering himself. In fact, "some good, some so-so odds and ends" seems more accurate, if the reader is talking about Martial's technical expertise. Granted, there are various subjects that certain readers would call "bad" or at least deeply offensive based purely on their subject matter: his obscenity, his mocking epigrams at the expense of people with three hairs or three teeth (although here even a casual reading should make clear that it's not that these people are mocked for their deformities but for their refusal to accept what their lives have become and continue to act as if they can still make themselves young and desirable), and his toadying to Domitian. About the latter, I would say this: I've avoided translating those epigrams, but I do understand why Martial wrote them, as would many English poets through the eighteenth century. Poets survived on patronage, and their poetry had to earn that patronage.

Translation can be a vexing problem if you let it be—or even if you don't. A bad translation or an inept translation does Martial a disservice. There are some things various translators have done with Martial that I would never do. I do not update Martial: his cart pulled by mules remains just that; it's neither a rickshaw nor a taxi cab; a caupona is neither a café nor a deli. I eschew anachronism altogether. There is only one instance of an anachronism in this book (IV.14), and that's Martial's own anachronism where, he writes, Catullus might dare to send his sparrow to the great Virgil, ignoring their birth and death dates. He does this because he is sending his own poems to the epic poet Silius Italicus and thus implicitly is comparing himself to Catullus. I try to keep the Latin names in the translations, but I'm willing to omit them. However, for the present book, Latin names are included, I believe, in all the translations where they appear in the original. There are poems that do not include names. My own method, hardly the stuff of a theoretical essay, is to stay as close to the original as I am able. However, I'm willing, on a poem by poem basis, to vary, add, omit, or substitute if it works for the individual poem and doesn't violate the spirit or the essential subject matter of the original.

R. L. Barth

To Martial

After your death, Pliny wrote praising you
For genius, satire, wit, and candor too.
Now, take this note across the centuries:
Tribute from one of your lesser legatees
Who, Pliny-like, would also recommend
Your poems, you—good company, good friend.

Contents

Book I

Book II

Book III

Book IV

Book V

Book I

I.1

Hic est quem legis ille, quem requiris,
toto notus in orbe Martialis
argutis epigrammaton libellis:
cui, lector studiose, quod dedisti
uiuenti decus atque sentienti,
rari post cineres habent poetae.

I.8

Quod magni Thraseae consummatique Catonis
    dogmata sic sequeris saluos ut esse uelis,
pectore nec nudo strictos incurris in ensis,
    quod fecisse uelim te, Deciane, facis.
Nolo uirum facili redemit qui sanguine famam,
    hunc uolo, laudari qui sine morte potest.

I.10

Petit Gemellus nuptias Maronillae
    et cupit et instat et precatur et donat.
Adeone pulchra est? Immo foedius nil est.
    Quid ergo in illa petitur et placet? Tussit.

I.16

Sunt bona, sunt quaedam mediocria, sunt mala plura
    quae legis hic: aliter non fit, Auite, liber.

I.1

Reader, behold! Here's Martial,
To whom the whole world's partial
For epigrams. For heaping
On him fame held in keeping
Mostly for the massed ranks you
Honor (the dead), he thanks you.

I.8

You follow teachings of Thrasea and
Virtuous Cato, but you take a stand
To save your life, not throwing it away
Exposed to drawn swords in some border fray.
Decianus, that's what I wish in fact.
I don't approve a man whose dying act
In battle brings to him undying fame.
I love one who, not dying, makes his name.

I.10

Maronilla's courted by Gemellus.
He lusts for her, pleads, gives her presents. Tell us,
How lovely . . . What, she's ugly? Then her cough'll
Give us a hint. It's positively awful.

I.16

Some good, some bad, some so-so odds and ends:
Thus a book's made, Avitus, my good friend.

I.20

Dic mihi, quis furor est? Turba spectante uocata
    solus boletos, Caeciliane, uoras.
Quid dignum tanto tibi uentre gulaque precabor?
    Boletum qualem Claudius edit, edas.

I.25

Ede tuos tandem populo, Faustine, libellos
    et cultum docto pectore profer opus,
quod nec Cecropiae damnent Pandionis arces
    nec sileant nostri praetereantque senes.
Ante fores stantem dubitas admittere Famam
    teque piget curae praemia ferre tuae?
Post te victurae per te quoque vivere chartae
    incipiant: cineri gloria sera venit.

I.27

Hesterna tibi nocte dixeramus,
quincunces puto post decem peractos,
cenares hodie, Procille, mecum.
Tu factam tibi rem statim putasti
et non sobria uerba subnotasti
exemplo nimium periculoso:
miso mnamona sumpotan, Procille.

I.20

Tell me, Caecilianus, what's this madness:
You gobble mushrooms, every one, at such a rate
I offer up this curse to your fat belly:
May you eat mushrooms like those Claudius ate.

I.25

Faustinus, publish; bring to light your skill,
And your acute mind, work that neither will
Be thumped by the Athenians critically
Nor be passed over by men silently.
Why keep Fame waiting, standing at your door?
Accept the praise for labors, if not more.
Your writings will outlive you; live in turn
Through them now; glory's late when offered to an urn.

I.27

Late last night, after fifty jars of wine,
I asked you if you'd care to dine
Today. You took me at my tipsy word,
Quietly hoarding what you heard—
Dangerous precedent! Procillus, please:
No one likes drunks with memories.

I.34

Incustoditis et apertis, Lesbia, semper
　　liminibus peccas nec tua furta tegis,
et plus spectator quam te delectat adulter
　　nec sunt grata tibi gaudia si qua latent.
At meretrix abigit testem ueloque seraque
　　raraque Submemmi fornice rima patet.
A Chione saltem uel ab Iade disce pudorem:
　　abscondunt spurcas et monumenta lupas.
Numquid dura tibi nimium censura uidetur?
　　deprendi ueto te, Lesbia, non futui.

I.53

Vna est in nostris tua, Fidentine, libellis
pagina, sed certa domini signata figura,
quae tua traducit manifesto carmina furto.
Sic interpositus uillo contaminat uncto
urbica Lingonicus Tyrianthina bardocucullus,
sic Arrentinae uiolant crystallina testae,
sic niger in ripis errat cum forte Caystri,
inter Ledaeos ridetur coruus olores,
sic ubi multisona feruet sacer Atthide lucus,
inproba Cecropias offendit pica querelas.
Indice non opus est nostris nec iudice libris,
stat contra dicitque tibi tua pagina 'Fur es.'

I.34

You like your sex at home with doors unguarded;
You get off having spectators rewarded.
No secret pleasures please. Consider whores:
They pull their curtains fast or bar their doors;
Suburban brothels have few chinks to see.
Learn from dead whores a little modesty:
Their tombs are airtight. Do I seem severe
With public censure in a poem here?
Lesbia, I'm not suggesting chastity,
But re-considering your secrecy.

I.53

Fidentinus, my book's one page
Is yours, but I won't even rage
So obviously you're a thief—
Just as a stola comes to grief
When city cloaks stain it with grease;
And when Arretine pots disgrace
Vases of crystal, and the crows
Give a noisy, scornful dose
Of laughter to Leda's swans; magpies
Mock nightingales, so for your lies,
That single page's poems insist
That you're a scurvy plagiarist.

I.62

Casta nec antiquis cedens Laevina Sabinis
  et quamvis tetrico tristior ipsa viro
dum modo Lucrino, modo se demittit Averno,
  et dum Baianis saepe fouetur aquis,
incidit in flammas: iuvenemque secuta relicto
  coniuge Penelope venit, abit Helene.

I.75

Dimidium donare Lino quam credere totum
  qui mauolt, mauolt perdere dimidium.

I.90

Quod numquam maribus iunctam te, Bassa, videbam
  quodque tibi moechum fabula nulla dabat,
omne sed officium circa te semper obibat
  turba tui sexus, non adeunte viro,
esse videbaris, fateor, Lucretia nobis:
  at tu, pro facinus, Bassa, fututor eras.
Inter se geminos audes committere cunnos
  mentiturque virum prodigiosa Venus.
Commenta es dignum Thebano aenigmate monstrum,
  hic ubi vir non est, ut sit adulterium.

I.62

Laevina, chaste as Sabines' status quo,
More rigid than her mate, would often go
Bathe in the Lucrine lake, sometimes Avernus,
And in the Baiaen baths fell in love's furnace.
She and her young stud packed their bags to flee.
Helen she left, who came Penelope.

I.75

He who lends Linus half but not all tosses
Away some money but still cuts his losses.

I.90

I've never seen you in the midst of men;
No rumors even link you to a lover.
Females surround you always, even when
You need some errands run. So, under cover,
Bassa, I thought you might be a Lucretia,
But no indeed: you have been fornicating.
Outrageously, you have contrived to leash a
Pussy to yet another pussy, mating
The two as your clit functions like a prick.
Thus you've contrived your own riddle-dee-dee
That rivals the Theban one. Now answer, quick,
How lack a man but have adultery?

I.109

Issa est passere nequior Catulli,
Issa est purior osculo columbae,
Issa est blandior omnibus puellis,
Issa est carior Indicis lapillis,
Issa est deliciae catella Publi.
Hanc tu, si queritur, loqui putabis;
sentit tristitiamque gaudiumque.
Collo nixa cubat capitque somnos,
ut suspiria nulla sentiantur;
et desiderio coacta uentris
gutta pallia non fefellit ulla,
sed blando pede suscitat toroque
deponi monet et rogat leuari.
Castae tantus inest pudor catellae,
ignorat Venerem; nec inuenimus
dignum tam tenera uirum puella.
Hanc ne lux rapiat suprema totam,
picta Publius exprimit tabella,
in qua tam similem uidebis Issam,
ut sit tam similis sibi nec ipsa.
Issam denique pone cum tabella:
aut utramque putabis esse ueram,
aut utramque putabis esse pictam.

I.113

Quaecumque lusi iuuenis et puer quodam
apinasque nostras, quas nec ipse iam noui,
male conlocare si bonas uoles horas
et inuidebis otio tuo, lector,
a Valeriano Pollio petes Quinto,
per quem perire non licet meis nugis.

I.109

More playful than the sparrow of Catullus,
Purer than a dove, more loving than
Any sweet maiden, dearer than gemstones:
That's Issa, the pet dog of Publius.
If she should whine, you'll swear that the dog's speaking.
She feels her master's sadness and his cheer.
She lies upon his neck; so quietly she sleeps
That you might wonder if she's even breathing.
She's thoroughly housebroken—with a nudge,
She tells her master she must go outdoors.
Modest, she's never had a suitor for
Publius never found a worthy mate.
Here's the picture Publius commissioned
So death not take her wholly; if you look
You'll see an Issa who out-Issa's Issa.
Place Issa and her picture side by side,
And you'll say both are live or both are painted.

I.113

Dear reader, if you'd spend some good time badly
And wreck your leisure time, then you can buy
The trifles even I've forgotten gladly
From Quintus Valerianus—I don't know why—
Who won't allow my juvenilia to die.

Book II

II.29

Rufe, uides illum subsellia prima terentem,
    cuius et hinc lucet sardonychata manus
quaeque Tyron totiens epotauere lacernae
    et toga non tactas uincere iussa niues,
cuius olet toto pinguis coma Marcelliano
    et splendent uolso bracchia trita pilo,
non hesterna sedet lunata lingula planta,
    coccina non laesum pingit aluta pedem,
et numerosa linunt stellantem splenia frontem.
    Ignoras quid sit? Splenia tolle, leges.

II.30

Mutua uiginti sestertia forte rogabam,
    quae uel donanti non graue munus erat:
quippe rogabatur felixque uetusque sodalis
    et cuius laxas arca flagellat opes.
Is mihi 'Diues eris, si causas egeris' inquit.
    Quod peto da, Gai: non peto consilium.

II.37

Quidquid ponitur hinc et inde uerris,
mammas suminis imbricemque porci
communemque duobus attagenam,
mullum dimidium lupumque totum
muraenaeque latus femurque pulli5
stillantemque alica sua palumbum.
Haec cum condita sunt madente mappa,
traduntur puero domum ferenda:
nos accumbimus otiosa turba.
Vllus si pudor est, repone cenam:
cras te, Caeciliane, non uocaui.

II.29
Rufus, look at those front seats! Do you see
That man whose purple cloak hangs past the knee;
Whose jewels dazzle, even to our row;
Whose well-scrubbed toga humbles purest snow;
Whose hair's so oiled it permeates the air
In the theater; whose arms've been plucked bare;
Whose laces bind red leather shoes, each ankle
Crescented; and whose starry face must rankle
The firmament? The meaning? Peel those stars,
Rufus; beauty marks hide the ex-slave's scars.

II.30
Caius, I ask a loan from you today.
Your money bags are bursting, but you say,
"You'll get rich taking up the law." Quite nice:
I ask for money, Caius, not advice.

II.37
Mullet, sow breast, pork, woodcock, a whole pike,
Some lamprey, chicken legs, pigeons in sauce:
You sweep the table of the foods you like,
Wrapping them in your napkin, to our loss.
Your servant lugs it home. Have you no shame,
Caecilianus? We've hardly had a bite.
That supper invitation in your name,
Sir, wasn't for tomorrow but tonight.

II.38

Quid mihi reddat ager quaeris, Line, Nomentanus?
    Hoc mihi reddit ager: te, Line, non uideo.

II.59

Mica uocor: quid sim cernis, cenatio parua:
    ex me Caesareum prospicis ecce tholum.
Frange toros, pete uina, rosas cape, tinguere nardo:
    ipse iubet mortis te meminisse deus.

II.67

Occurris quocumque loco mihi, Postume, clamas
    protinus et prima est haec tua uox 'Quid agis?'
Hoc, si me decies una conueneris hora,
    dicis: habes puto tu, Postume, nil quod agas.

II.70

Non uis in solio prius lauari
quemquam, Cotile: causa quae, nisi haec est,
undis ne fouearis irrumatis?
Primus te licet abluas: necesse est
ante hic mentula quam caput lauetur.

II.80

Hostem cum fugeret, se Fannius ipse peremit.
    Hic, rogo, non furor est, ne moriare, mori?

II.38

You ask me what my farmlands yield?
Well, this: Linus, you're far afield.

II.59

"Morsel," I'm called, the little dining room
That overlooks Augustus's domed tomb.
Anoint yourself; bring wine; wear roses. See!
The god reminds you of mortality.

II.67

Posthumus, when we meet you holler out,
"How do you do?" No matter, sir, if you
Meet me ten times an hour, it's just the same.
Here's my conclusion: you've not much to do.

II.70

Cotilus, none may bathe before you do.
You won't bathe in that rank pollution? Brace
Yourself for what you've seemingly neglected:
You'll have to wash your prick before your face.

II.80

Fannius ran from battle
And, while his feet were flying,
Took his own life. What madness:
To die for fear of dying.

II.83
Foedasti miserum, marite, moechum,
et se, qui fuerant prius, requirunt
trunci naribus auribusque uoltus.
Credis te satis esse uindicatum?
Erras: iste potest et irrumare.

II.83
Catching the cuckhold, you unsheathed your knife
And went to work on him who screwed your wife,
Lopping his nose and ears. Pure vengeance gained?
No, one of his appendages remained.

Book III

III.9

Versiculos in me narratur scribere Cinna:
    Non scribit, cuius carmina nemo legit.

III.10

Constituit, Philomuse, pater tibi milia bina
menstrua perque omnis praestitit illa dies,
luxuriam premeret cum crastina semper egestas
et uitiis essent danda diurna tuis.
Idem te moriens heredem ex asse reliquit:
exheredauit te, Philomuse, pater.

III.18

Perfrixisse tuas questa est praefatio fauces:
    cum te excusaris, Maxime, quid recitas?

III.26

Praedia solus habes et solus, Candide, nummos,
    aurea solus habes, murrina solus habes,
Massica solus habes et Opimi Caecuba solus,
    et cor solus habes, solus et ingenium.
Omnia solus habes ‹ nec me puta uelle negare
    uxorem sed habes, Candide, cum populo.

III.33

Ingenuam malo, sed si tamen illa negetur,
libertina mihi proxuma condicio est.
Extremo est ancilla loco: sed uincet utramque,
si facie nobis haec erit ingenua.

III.9
Cinna attacks me in his verse, it's said.
But does he write, whose poems aren't ever read?

III.10
Two thousand every month, doled day by day,
Your father gave, knowing just how you blew it.
He tried to check extravagance his way.
But now he's dead; and though he surely knew it,
Philomusus, sole heir when the will's read,
You'll find yourself soon disinherited.

III.18
You've pleaded that your throat was sore.
Excused, Maximus, why say more?

III.26
You own your farms alone, your cash alone,
Your gold and murrhine goblets, wines; you own,
Candidus, likewise heart, wit, property.
Only your wife's a shared commodity.

III.33
I'd rather have a lady, but if denied
Then a freedwoman would be my next choice.
My last resort—though swallowing my pride—
Would be a slave, but if she moves with poise
And if she's beautiful—that counts as worth—
I'd take her, beauty triumphs over birth.

III.35

Artis Phidiacae toreuma clarum
pisces aspicis: adde aquam, natabunt.

III.51

Cum faciem laudo, cum miror crura manusque,
   dicere, Galla, soles "Nuda placebo magis",
et semper uitas communia balnea nobis.
   Numquid, Galla, times ne tibi non placeam?

III.54

Cum dare non possim quod poscis, Galla, rogantem,
   multo simplicius, Galla, negare potes.

III.71

Mentula cum doleat puero, tibi, Naeuole, culus,
   non sum diuinus, sed scio quid facias.

III.72

Vis futui nec vis mecum, Saufeia, lavari.
   Nescio quod magnum suspicor esse nefas.
Aut tibi pannosae dependent pectore mammae,
   aut sulcos uteri prodere nuda times,
aut infinito lacerum patet inguen hiatu,
   aut aliquid cunni prominet ore tui.
Sed nihil est horum, credo; pulcherrima nuda es.
   Si uerum est, uitium peius habes: fatua es.

III.35

In clear relief, Phidias wrought these fish.
Add water; watch them swim around the dish.

III.51

I praise your face, your legs, your hands; and when I do
You say, "I'd please you more if nude." But you,
Galla, avoid the baths in which I sport.
You think I'll come up short?

III.54

No, Galla, I don't have your asking fee.
Let's simplify: say "no" immediately.

III.71

Naevolus, your boy's ass is sore; your prick is too.
Although I am no seer, I know just what you do.

III.72

Saufi, you think the two of us should hook up,
And yet, come bathing time, you seem to cook up
Excuses not to bathe together. Why?
Some blemish? A furrowed belly to belie
Your image? Are your small tits wrinkled, sagging?
Your body used up? Tumor to set me gagging?
Nonsense. You're lovely naked; but come, come,
For all your beauty, you've one flaw: you're dumb.

III.76

Arrigis ad uetulas, fastidis, Basse, puellas,
    nec formonsa tibi, sed moritura placet.
Hic, rogo, non furor est, non haec est mentula demens?
    Cum possis Hecaben, non potes Andromachen!

III.76
Bassus, it's the old hags who light your fire;
Young girls earn your contempt, not your desire.
Madman, this sexual insanity:
To love Hecuba, spurn Andromache.

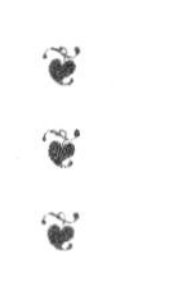

Book IV

IV.5

Vir bonus et pauper linguaque et pectore uerus,
    quid tibi uis urbem qui, Fabiane, petis?
Qui nec leno potes nec comissator haberi,
    nec pauidos tristi uoce citare reos,
nec potes uxores cari corrumpere amici,
    nec potes algentes arrigere ad uetulas,
uendere nec uanos circa Palatia fumos,
    plaudere nec Cano, plaudere nec Glaphyro:
unde miser uiues? — "Homo certus, fidus amicus." —
    Hoc nihil est: numquam sic Philomelus eris.

IV.11

Dum nimium uano tumefactus nomine gaudes
    et Saturninum te, miser, esse pudet,
impia Parrhasia mouisti bella sub ursa,
    qualia qui Phariae coniugis arma tulit.
Excideratne adeo fatum tibi nominis huius,
    obruit Actiaci quod grauis ira freti?
An tibi promisit Rhenus quod non dedit illi
    Nilus, et Arctois plus licuisset aquis?
Ille etiam nostris Antonius occidit armis,
    qui tibi conlatus, perfide, Caesar erat.

IV.5

Fabianus, sincere, honest and poor,
You've come to Rome. What're you searching for?
No pander, nor kiss-ass, you won't browbeat
Helpless defendants; no huckster of deceit
Seducing a close friend's wife; chaser after
Bloodless old bags; sweller of cheers and laughter
Fringing musicians; nor influence-monger:
How will you earn a living? "There's no stronger,
More loyal friend or . . ." Stop! Rome's ethical
Never amount to anything at all.

IV.11

While bloated by your sense of self-importance
And yet ashamed that you weren't more renowned,
You instigated an all-out rebellion
In Upper Germany, turning your legions
Against Domitian and the state of Rome,
Declaring war like he who took up arms
For his Egyptian consort. Did you forget
The raging sea at Actium? Or think
The Rhine would give you what the Nile refused him?
Antony was felled by Roman arms,
But, Saturninus, even Antony,
Set against you, you traitor, was a Caesar.

IV.14

Sili, Castalidum decus sororum,
qui periuria barbari furoris
ingenti premis ore perfidosque
astus Hannibalis leuisque Poenos
magnis cedere cogis Africanis:
paulum seposita seueritate,
dum blanda uagus alea December
incertis sonat hinc et hinc fritillis
et ludit tropa nequiore talo,
nostris otia commoda Camenis,
nec torua lege fronte, sed remissa
lasciuis madidos iocis libellos.
Sic forsan tener ausus est Catullus
magno mittere Passerem Maroni.

IV.24

Omnes quas habuit, Fabiane, Lycoris amicas
    extulit: uxori fiat amica meae.

IV.33

Plena laboratis habeas cum scrinia libris,
    emittis quare, Sosibiane, nihil?
"Edent heredes" inquis "mea carmina". Quando?
    Tempus erat iam te, Sosibiane, legi.

IV.14

Silius Italicus, the Muses' glory,
Who wrote in epic song of Hannibal,
His pride and faithless Carthaginians
Humbled and yielding to our Scipios,
Please lay aside awhile your gravitas
For Saturnalia's wilder games of chance;
And pray indulge my muse and read with humor
My little books with all their impudence.
In just this way might our Catullus dare
To send his sparrow to the greater Virgil.

IV.24

Lycoris, all your friends are buried.
Care to befriend the girl I married?

IV.33

Your manuscripts are stacked, bookcases groan,
And yet you've published nothing of your own.
"My heirs will publish . . ." What? After you're dead?
Sosibianus, it's past time you're read.

IV.44

Hic est pampineis uiridis modo Vesbius umbris,
    presserat hic madidos nobilis uua lacus:
haec iuga quam Nysae colles plus Bacchus amauit;
    hoc nuper Satyri monte dedere choros;
haec Veneris sedes, Lacedaemone gratior illi;
    hic locus Herculeo nomine clarus erat.
Cuncta iacent flammis et tristi mersa fauilla:
    nec superi uellent hoc licuisse sibi.

IV.49

Nescit, crede mihi, quid sint epigrammata, Flacce,
qui tantum lusus illa iocosque uocat.
Ille magis ludit qui scribit prandia saeui
Tereos aut cenam, crude Thyesta, tuam,
aut puero liquidas aptantem Daedalon alas,
pascentem Siculas aut Polyphemon ouis.
A nostris procul est omnis uesica libellis,
Musa nec insano syrmate nostra tumet.
"Illa tamen laudant omnes, mirantur, adorant".
Confiteor: laudant illa, sed ista legunt.

IV.44

Vesuvius, once green with leafy vines,
Where barrels overflowed once with your wines;
Heights Bacchus loved more than the Nysan hill;
On whose slopes satyrs frolicked; Venus still
Had her abode, loved more than Sparta; land he,
Hercules, gave fame through divinity.
Now fires and ashes smother cities, fields,
And gods lament the powers that they wield.

IV.49

Flaccus, I swear that man's an ignoramus
Who calls the epigram a trifling joke.
He trifles more who sings the savage meal
Of Tereus; or the banquet of Thyestes;
Or Daedalus outfitting melting wings;
Or Polyphemus pasturing his sheep.
Far from my little books be all such bombast;
My Muse is swollen with no tragic frenzy.
"You know that all men worship tragedies?"
That's true, but all men read my epigrams.

IV.66

Egisti uitam semper, Line, municipalem,
  qua nihil omnino uilius esse potest.
Idibus et raris togula est excussa Kalendis,
  duxit et aestates synthesis una decem.
Saltus aprum, campus leporem tibi misit inemptum,
  silua grauis turdos exagitata dedit,
captus flumineo uenit de gurgite piscis,
  uina ruber fudit non peregrina cadus.
Nec tener Argolica missus de gente minister,
  sed stetit inculti rustica turba foci.
Vilica uel duri conpressa est nupta coloni,
  incaluit quotiens saucia uena mero.
Nec nocuit tectis ignis nec Sirius agris,
  nec mersa est pelago nec fuit ulla ratis.
Subposita est blando numquam tibi tessera talo,
  alea sed parcae sola fuere nuces.
Dic ubi sit decies, mater quod auara reliquit.
  Nusquam est: fecisti rem, Line, difficilem.

IV.71

Quaero diu totam, Safroni Rufe, per urbem,
  si qua puella neget: nulla puella negat.
Tamquam fas non sit, tamquam sit turpe negare,
  tamquam non liceat, nulla puella negat.
Casta igitur nulla est? Sunt castae mille. Quid ergo
  casta facit? Non dat, non tamen illa negat.

IV.66

You've always loved the countryside,
Where living's cheap. Out there, at Ides
Or the odd Kalends, you unfold
A toga that's ten summers' old!
Forests dole boars; woods, hare; and brush,
When beaten, plumpest quail and thrush.
Rivers spawn fish for baitless lines.
Earthenware pours your homegrown wines.
The peasant, not the Greek slave boy,
Tends the hearth fire in your employ
While you seduce such women there—
Farmers' and stewards' wives—no care
But satisfaction. Well-plowed fields,
Safe from dog days, sprout bumper yields;
Your villa's secure; no galleys sink
In the deep sea; nor would you think
Exchanging knucklebones for dice
And steeper antes worth the price.
Where's cash from mother's wondrous will,
Then, Linus? Gone? More wondrous still.

IV.71

I searched all Rome for one girl who says no.
No one says no. You'd think to move the jaw
That way a shame, disgrace, against the law.
No one says no, Rufus, but you'll say, "Whoa!
Surely some must be chaste?" Thousands, I'd guess.
Mind you, they don't say no—just don't say yes.

IV.72

Exigis ut donem nostros tibi, Quinte, libellos.
    Non habeo, sed habet bibliopola Tryphon.
"Aes dabo pro nugis et emam tua carmina sanus?
    Non, inquis, faciam tam fatue." Nec ego.

IV.77

Numquam diuitias deos rogaui
contentus modicis meoque laetus:
paupertas, ueniam dabis, recede.
Causast quae subiti nouique uoti?
Pendentem uolo Zoilum uidere.

IV.81

Epigramma nostrum cum Fabulla legisset,
negare nullam quo queror puellarum,
semel rogata bisque terque neglexit
preces amantis. Iam, Fabulla, promitte:
negare iussi, pernegare non iussi.

IV.89

Ohe, iam satis est, ohe, libelle,
iam peruenimus usque ad umbilicos.
Tu procedere adhuc et ire quaeris,
nec summa potes in schida teneri,
sic tamquam tibi res peracta non sit,
quae prima quoque pagina peracta est.
Iam lector queriturque deficitque,
iam librarius hoc et ipse dicit
"Ohe, iam satis est, ohe, libelle."

IV.72

Quintus, you ask me for my book, but I
Don't have an extra copy; you could buy . . .
"Money for trifles when I'm sober? No!
I'll not do something so absurd!" Ditto.

IV.77

I never begged the gods for wealth before,
Content with all I owned, although thought poor.
Now, Poverty, begone; gods bring me cash.
Neither hypocritical nor brash,
My prayer has one design, and that's to see
Zoilus, turned green, hang himself from a tree.

IV.81

I wrote a poem saying no girls say no.
Fabulla read it and turned down her lover
Three times. Point taken, girl, but even so
Say yes; I didn't say, "Say no forever."

IV.89

Hey, little book, you've reached the parchment's end!
Ignoring limits still, you keep on prattling on.
The first page was sufficient. Why pretend
That I or any reader wants you rattling on?
The reader's out of patience, pert contrarian.
"Enough, in truth!" cries even the librarian.

Book V

V.14

Sedere primo solitus in gradu semper
tunc, cum liceret occupare, Nanneius
bis excitatus terque transtulit castra,
et inter ipsas paene tertius sellas
post Gaiumque Luciumque consedit.
Illinc cucullo prospicit caput tectus
oculoque ludos spectat indecens uno;
et hinc miser deiectus in uiam transit,
subsellioque semifultus extremo
et male receptus altero genu iactat
equiti sedere Leitoque se stare.

V.18

Quod tibi Decembri mense, quo uolant mappae
gracilesque ligulae cereique chartaeque
et acuta senibus testa cum Damascenis,
praeter libellos uernulas nihil misi,
fortasse auarus uidear aut inhumanus.
Odi dolosas munerum et malas artes;
imitantur hamos dona: namque quis nescit
auidum uorata decipi scarum musca?
Quotiens amico diuiti nihil donat,
o Quintiane, liberalis est pauper.

V.14

He always occupied a front row seat
When seizing it was lawful; now, defeat
Awaits Nanneius, quickly put to rout.
From the front row, he shifts his camp about,
Then hunkers down between and just behind
Lucius and Gaius, fashioning a kind
Of third seat where, head cowled, slyly, one-eyed,
He watches the performance until, spied,
He's routed once again. Then up the ramp,
Half-propped on bench and half on knees that cramp
He seems to sit when knights look over, and
When the attendants stare, he seems to stand.

V.18

Quintianus, December comes,
And presents fly: crocks of dried plums
Imported from Damascus, papers,
Shoe laces, napkins, and wax tapers.
Sending only the books I write,
Do I seem stingy? Impolite?
I hate gifts given cunningly,
Like fishhooks, for who cannot see
How bream are suckered by the bait?
Though he gives nothing to the Great,
The poor man, every time he does,
Is simply being generous.

V.29

Si quando leporem mittis mihi, Gellia, dicis:
    "Formonsus septem, Marce, diebus eris."
Si non derides, si uerum, lux mea, narras,
    edisti numquam, Gellia, tu leporem.

V.42

Callidus effracta nummos fur auferet arca,
    prosternet patrios impia flamma lares;
debitor usuram pariter sortemque negabit,
    non reddet sterilis semina iacta seges;
dispensatorem fallax spoliabit amica,
    mercibus extructas obruet unda rates.
Extra fortunam est quidquid donatur amicis:
    quas dederis solas semper habebis opes.

V.47

Numquam se cenasse domi Philo iurat, et hoc est:
    non cenat, quotiens nemo uocauit eum.

V.59

Quod non argentum, quod non tibi mittimus aurum,
    hoc facimus causa, Stella diserte, tua.
Quisquis magna dedit, uoluit sibi magna remitti;
    fictibus nostris exoneratus eris.

V.29

You, whenever sending me a hare, say
"You'll be handsome for seven days. It's true."
If you're not jesting, Gellia, then I dare say
You've never eaten hare yourself, have you?

V.42

A thief may break in, steal your money;
A fire destroy your ancient home;
Your debtor declare bankruptcy;
Your fields turn barren, not repaying
Even the cost of seeds you scattered;
A courtesan may roll your steward;
Your laden ships may sink at sea;
But what you give to friends eludes
Grasping Dame Fortune; truly, sir,
Riches you give away to friends
Are the ones you'll have forever.

V.47

You never dine at home? That's quite a feat,
Philo, but frequently you just don't eat.

V.59

Sending you neither gold nor silver dishes,
Stella, I've exercised much care.
Great gifts have greater ones behind great wishes.
Accept this earthenware.

V.68

Arctoa de gente comam tibi, Lesbia, misi,
    ut scires quanto sit tua flaua magis.

V.69

Antoni Phario nihil obiecture Pothino
    et leuius tabula quam Cicerone nocens,
quid gladium demens Romana stringis in ora?
    hoc admisisset nec Catilina nefas.
Impius infando miles corrumpitur auro,
    et tantis opibus uox tacet una tibi.
Quid prosunt sacrae pretiosa silentia linguae?
    Incipient omnes pro Cicerone loqui.

V.73

Non donem tibi cur meos libellos
oranti totiens et exigenti
miraris, Theodore? Magna causa est:
dones tu mihi ne tuos libellos.

V.81

Semper pauper eris, si pauper es, Aemiliane:
    dantur opes nullis nunc nisi diuitibus.

V.68

I send these locks from Upper Germany.
You're blonder, Lesbia, as we can see.

V.69

O Anthony, do not reproach Pothinus
For killing Pompey when you have done worse
In murdering great Cicero, worse deed
Than all of your proscription lists. Madman,
Why draw the sword against the mouth of Rome,
Wickedness beyond even Cataline?
Corrupted by your gold, a legionary
Silenced a single voice; but of what use
Is the suppression of such eloquence?
The world will ever speak for Cicero.

V.73

You wonder why, despite your constant pleading,
I've never given you my verse?
Theodorus, you don't want mine for reading
But as excuse to give me yours.

V.81

If you're poor now, then you'll stay poor.
Emil, only the rich get more.

V.83

Insequeris, fugio; fugis, insequor. Haec mihi mens est:
uelle tuum nolo, Dindyme, nolle uolo.

V.84

Iam tristis nucibus puer relictis
clamoso reuocatur a magistro,
et blando male proditus fritillo,
arcana modo raptus e popina,
aedilem rogat udus aleator.
Saturnalia transiere tota,
nec munuscula parua nec minora
misisti mihi, Galla, quam solebas.
Sane sic abeat meus December:
scis certe, puto, uestra iam uenire
Saturnalia, Martias Kalendas;
tunc reddam tibi, Galla, quod dedisti.

V.83

Dindymus,
When you pursue, I fly;
You fly, and I pursue.
That which you wish, I don't;
What you don't wish, I do.

V.84

The boy now leaves his playthings, heeds the call
Of bawling teachers while the drunken gambler,
Betrayed by bones and hauled off from some tavern,
Begs mercy of the magistrate; and so,
Galla, our Saturnalia ends this year.
You never sent the small nor cheaper presents
You always gave. As our December's over,
You know, of course, your Saturnalia nears.
March closes in. Galla, you can expect
Presents to equal what you've given me.

Book VI

VI.19

Non de ui neque caede nec ueneno,
sed lis est mihi de tribus capellis:
uicini queror has abesse furto.
Hoc iudex sibi postulat probari:
tu Cannas Mithridaticumque bellum
et periuria Punici furoris
et Sullas Mariosque Muciosque
magna uoce sonas manuque tota.
Iam dic, Postume, de tribus capellis.

VI.25

Marcelline, boni suboles sincera parentis,
    horrida Parrhasio quem tegit ursa iugo,
ille uetus pro te patriusque quid optet amicus
    accipe et haec memori pectore uota tene:
causa sit ut uirtus nec te temerarius ardor
    in medios enses saeuaque tela ferat.
Bella uellint Martemque ferum rationis egentes,
    tu potes et patris miles et esse ducis.

VI.32

Cum dubitaret adhuc belli ciuilis Enyo
    forsitan et posset uincere mollis Otho,
damnauit multo staturum sanguine Martem
    et fodit certa pectora tota manu.
Sit Cato, dum uiuit, sane uel Caesare maior:
    dum moritur, numquid maior Othone fuit?

VI.19

Come on, Posthumus, when I paid my fee,
I thought I hired a lawyer who would sue
The neighbor who absconded with three goats.
There's no assault or rape, no battery.
Simple? Just prove it to the judge? Oh, no,
With purple prose and a bad actor's gestures,
You rant of Cannae, the Mithridatic war,
Those lying, frenzied Carthaginians,
Sulla, and Marius. Come on, Posthumus,
Just tell the judge about my stolen goats.

VI.25

Marcellinus, son of a worthy father,
As you deploy into the frozen North,
Listen to me, your old friend and your father's:
I wish—please keep my prayers in your heart—
That you'll be brave, of course, but not foolhardy;
Your valor disciplined when you're in battle.
Let men who lack all reason wish for war
And savagery, but you can be the soldier
Both of your father and your emperor.

VI.32

Civil war raging, Bellona undecided
Watched closely; Otho, who might hold the throne,
Despaired to see the Roman blood that flowed
And, resolved, plunged the sword into his chest.
Say Cato when alive outshone great Caesar;
Was he a greater man in death than Otho?

VI.33

Nil miserabilius, Matho, pedicone Sabello
    uidisti, quo nil laetius ante fuit.
Furta, fugae, mortes seruorum, incendia, luctus
    adfligunt hominem, iam miser et futuit

VI.34

Basia da nobis, Diadumene, pressa. "Quot?" inquis.
    Oceani fluctus me numerare iubes
et maris Aegaei sparsas per litora conchas
    et quae Cecropio monte uagantur apes,
quaeque sonant pleno uocesque manusque theatro
    cum populus subiti Caesaris ora uidet.
Nolo quot arguto dedit exorata Catullo
    Lesbia: pauca cupit qui numerare potest.

VI.48

Quod tam grande sophos clamat tibi turba togata,
    non tu, Pomponi, cena diserta tua est.

VI.60

Laudat, amat, cantat nostros mea Roma libellos,
    meque sinus omnes, me manus omnis habet.
Ecce rubet quidam, pallet, stupet, oscitat, odit.
    Hoc uolo: nunc nobis carmina nostra placent.

VI.33

What man's more wretched than the sodomite Sabellus,
Matho, at one time joyous? Now, they tell us,
Thefts, deaths, escaped slaves, fires, and griefs exert such force
The wretched man has normal intercourse.

VI.34

Diadumenus, give me kisses. "How many?"
Why not just have me count the ocean waves,
The seashells strewn on the Aegean shores,
The bees on Attic Hybla, or the cheers
That echo through the jam-packed theater
When people see the figure of Domitian.
I want far more than Lesbia bestowed,
After he pleaded, on that witty Catullus.
He only wants a few if he can count them.

Martial's original has 'Caesaris', but the emperor at this time was Domitian.

VI.48

Pomponius, your clients' cheers are meant
Not for your speech; your dinner's eloquent.

VI.60

Rome praises, loves, and sings my little verses;
They're in all hands, all pockets, and all purses.
Look there! One blushes, pales, gasps, yawns, and curses.
That's what I want! I'm happy with my verses.

VI.65

"Hexametris epigramma facis" scio dicere Tuccam.
Tucca, solet fieri, denique, Tucca, licet.
"Sed tamen hoc longum est." Solet hoc quoque, Tucca, licetque:
si breuiora probas, disticha sola legas.
Conueniat nobis ut fas epigrammata longa
sit transire tibi, scribere, Tucca, mihi.

VI.70

Sexagesima, Marciane, messis
acta est et, puto, iam secunda Cottae
nec se taedia lectuli calentis
expertum meminit die uel uno.
Ostendit digitum, sed inpudicum,
Alconti Dasioque Symmachoque.
At nostri bene computentur anni
et quantum tetricae tulere febres
aut languor grauis aut mali dolores
a uita meliore separetur:
infantes sumus et senes uidemur.
Aetatem Priamique Nestorisque
longam qui putat esse, Marciane,
multum decipiturque falliturque.
Non est uiuere, sed ualere uita est.

VI.79

Tristis es et felix. Sciat hoc Fortuna caueto:
    ingratum dicet te, Lupe, si scierit.

VI.65

So Tucca says I'm writing in hexameters.
Well, there are precedents; it's quite legitimate.
But this one's very lengthy, Tucca, you complain.
Length has its precedents; it's quite legitimate.
If you okay my shorter ones, then read my couplets.
Let's make a pact: I'm free to write long epigrams,
And you feel equally as free to simply skip them.

VI.70

Cotta's some sixty-two years old
And never even had a cold
Nor spent a day in a sickbed.
With a deep frown, he quickly sped
His doctors to a distant place.
If we could accurately trace
Our years, subtract our illnesses,
Our fevers, all of our distresses
From our few happy, healthy days—
And, no, I don't mean this in praise—
We'd seem like infants, though in truth
We're old men very far from youth.
Think Priam, Nestor lived long lives?
No, you're mistaken: life derives
Not merely from inhaling air
But being free of sickly care.

VI.79

Lupus, despite your blessings
You're a mopey one.
You'd best take care: if Fortune
Sees you, you're undone.

VI.82

Quidam me modo, Rufe, diligenter
inspectum, uelut emptor aut lanista,
cum uoltu digitoque subnotasset,
"Tune es, tune" ait "ille Martialis,
cuius nequitias iocosque nouit
aurem qui modo non habet Batauam?"
Subrisi modice, leuique nutu
me quem dixerat esse non negaui.
"Cur ergo" inquit "habes malas lacernas?"
Respondi: "quia sum malus poeta."
Hoc ne saepius accidat poetae,
mittas, Rufe, mihi bonas lacernas.

VI.84

Sanus, cum solutas ambulet Philippus,
    octaphoro, Avite, baiulatur.
Hunc si sanum, Avite, non putabis,
    sanus, Avite, non eris.

VI.82

A fellow giving me the eye—
Arena-stocker out to buy?
Slave-trader?—when he'd taken note,
Said, "Pardon me, aren't you that Martial
To whom all men of taste're partial?"
I smiled discreetly, cleared my throat,
Nodded, mumbled, "The very same."
"Then why the shoddy cloak? For shame!"
I answered, "Well, I'm a poor poet."
Rufus, it was embarrassing!
If you'd not have this happening
Again, send me new clothes to show it.

VI.84

Philippus, healthy and without a pain,
Is carried in a litter by eight men.
Avitus, if you think him sane, why then,
Avitus, you yourself must be insane.

VI.85

Editur en sextus sine te mihi, Rufe Camoni,
    nec te lectorem sperat, amice, liber:
impia Cappadocum tellus et numine laeuo
    uisa tibi cineres reddit et ossa patri.
Funde tuo lacrimas orbata Bononia Rufo,
    et resonet tota planctus in Aemilia:
heu qualis pietas, heu quam breuis occidit aetas!
    uiderat Alphei praemia quinta modo.
Pectore tu memori nostros euoluere lusus,
    tu solitus totos, Rufe, tenere iocos,
accipe cum fletu maesti breue carmen amici
    atque haec absentis tura fuisse puta.

VI.91

Sancta ducis summi prohibet censura uetatque
    moechari. Gaude, Zoile, non futuis.

VI.85

My sixth book, Rufus, journeys forth without you,
Hopeless you'll read, for it knows all about you:
How impious Cappadocian lands return
Your father ash and bone inside an urn.
Let the Aemilian Way resonate
With lamentations of your widow's fate!
Alas! What virtue, what brief life has ended!
It saw but five Olympiads contended.
Rufus, you held my epigrams by heart
And quoted them; once more receive my art,
Your sorrowing friend's tribute going hence,
His distant offering, holy incense.

VI.91

Domitian publicly
Outlawed adultery.
Cocksuckers need not fear.
Zoilus, you're in the clear.

Book VII

VII.17

Ruris bibliotheca delicati,
uicinam uidet unde lector urbem,
inter carmina sanctiora si quis
lasciuae fuerit locus Thaliae,
hos nido licet inseras uel imo,
septem quos tibi misimus libellos
auctoris calamo sui notatos:
haec illis pretium facit litura.
At tu munere, delicata, paruo
quae cantaberis orbe nota toto,
pignus pectoris hoc mei tuere,
Iuli bibliotheca Martialis.

VII.23

Phoebe, ueni, sed quantus eras cum bella tonanti
    ipse dares Latiae plectra secunda lyrae.
Quid tanta pro luce precer? Tu, Polla, maritum
    saepe colas et se sentiat ille coli.

VII.25

Dulcia cum tantum scribas epigrammata semper
et cerussata candidiora cute,
nullaque mica salis nec amari fellis in illis
gutta sit, o demens, uis tamen illa legi!
Nec cibus ipse iuuat morsu fraudatus aceti,
nec grata est facies cui gelasinus abest.
Infanti melimela dato fatuasque mariscas:
nam mihi, quae nouit pungere, Chia sapit.

VII.17

Library of my good friend's country villa,
From whence, look up! you see the neighboring town,
If, among your weighty tomes, there's room
For Thalia, my wanton muse, no matter
If on the lowest shelf, I'm sending you
My seven books corrected by my hand,
Corrections that enhance the volumes' worth.
Library of dear Julius Martialis
To whom I dedicate my little present,
You'll be renowned beyond the Roman world.
Please guard these tokens of my deep affection.

VII.23

Phoebus, return as when you gave the second quill
To Lucan, singer of harsh war. Today,
On his birthdate, I wish you, dearest Polla, still
May venerate your husband's shade, and may
He know the veneration you display.

VII.25

Your epigrams are sweet, spotless as leaded skin;
There's neither salt nor drops of bitter gall within.
And yet, you silly man, you think that they'll be read.
Food that lacks good seasoning's served up with dread.
No face's lovely without dimples; give to boys
Your honey-apples, luscious figs, these sugared toys.
Your sweetly tasting epigrams just might be placed
At the bookstall, but Chian figs are to my taste.

VII.43

Primum est ut praestes, si quid te, Cinna, rogabo;
    illud deinde sequens ut cito, Cinna, neges.
Diligo praestantem; non odi, Cinna, negantem:
    sed tu nec praestas nec cito, Cinna, negas.

VII.46

Commendare tuum dum uis mihi carmine munus
Maeonioque cupis doctius ore loqui,
excrucias multis pariter me teque diebus,
et tua de nostro, Prisce, Thalia tacet.
Diuitibus poteris musas elegosque sonantes
mittere: pauperibus munera breui dato.

VII.70

Ipsarum tribadum tribas, Philaeni,
    recte, quam futuis, uocas amicam.

VII.76

Quod te diripiunt potentiores
per conuiuia, porticus, theatra,
et tecum, quotiens ita incidisti,
gestari iuuat, et iuuat lauari:
nolito nimium tibi placere.
Delectas, Philomuse, non amaris.

VII.43

Do me a favor, Cinna, if I request
Some favor, give it to me straight away;
Or else if you refuse, do so at once.
I love quick givers, don't hate quick deniers.
You're neither, Cinna, you're a ditherer.

VII.46

Priscus, while you'd commend your gift in verse
With Homer's skill, knowing your Muse is terse,
You've harassed me for weeks now. She's still dumb;
And I think, "Will my present ever come?"
Send wealthy patrons high-flown elegies.
For poor men, gifts with simple prose will please.

VII.70

Philaenis, dyke, you chase her for her gender,
And then you fuck her, flaunt her, and girlfriend her.

VII.76

Philomusus, hurry to feasts
And strolls along the porticoes,
Share great men's litters and their baths,
Their theater seats; and yet, Jove knows,
It's not your inner qualities.
No, you amuse them by degrees.

VII.96

Conditus hic ego sum Bassi dolor, Vrbicus infans,
    cui genus et nomen maxima Roma dedit.
Sex mihi de prima derant trieteride menses,
    ruperunt tetricae cum male pensa deae.
Quid species, quid lingua mihi, quid profuit aetas?
    da lacrimas tumulo, qui legis ista, meo:
sic ad Lethaeas, nisi Nestore serior, undas
    non eat, optabis quem superesse tibi.

VII.96

Here I, Urbicus, lie forever.
Great Rome gave both my birth and name.
Now Bassus mourns my too short life.
Six months before my third birthday,
Those harsh Fates cut my fatal thread.
My beauty, babble, tender years
Guaranteed no longer life.
When you read my inscription, shed
A tear, and so may your own child
Outlive you and avoid black Lethe
Until he's outlived Nestor's years.

Book VIII

VIII.1
Laurigeros domini, liber, intrature penates
disce uerecundo sanctius ore loqui.
Nuda recede Venus; non est tuus iste libellus:
tu mihi, tu Pallas Caesariana, ueni.

VIII.3
"Quinque satis fuerant: nam sex septemue libelli
est nimium: quid adhuc ludere, Musa, iuuat?
Sit pudor et finis: iam plus nihil addere nobis
fama potest: teritur noster ubique liber;
et cum rupta situ Messallae saxa iacebunt
altaque cum Licini marmora puluis erunt,
me tamen ora legent et secum plurimus hospes
ad patrias sedes carmina nostra feret."
Finieram, cum sic respondit nona sororum,
cui coma et unguento sordida uestis erat:
"Tune potes dulcis, ingrate, relinquere nugas?
dic mihi, quid melius desidiosus ages?
an iuuat ad tragicos soccum transferre coturnos
aspera uel paribus bella tonare modis,
praelegat ut tumidus rauca te uoce magister,
oderit et grandis uirgo bonusque puer?
Scribant ista graues nimium nimiumque seueri,
quos media miseros nocte lucerna uidet;
at tu Romano lepidos sale tingue libellos:
adgnoscat mores uita legatque suos.
Angusta cantare licet uidearis auena,
dum tua multorum uincat auena tubas."

VIII.1

My book, as you approach Domitian's palace,
Learn to speak modestly and reverently.
Begone rude Venus: this book's not for you.
Pallas, whom He adores, please come to me.

VIII.3

"Okay, five books—but really, six or seven?
That's surely overkill, dear Muse. I mean it.
Let's make an end of making all these books.
Everyone knows my name and reads my works.
Massala's stone-wrought sepulcher and even
Licinius' marble tomb will crumble,
And yet I'll still be read and visitors
Will buy and take my books to far-flung lands."
Thus, my conclusion, when my Thalia,
Her hair and garments trailing sweet perfumes,
Took me to task: "Ungrateful man, what's this?
Lay aside your trifles, do, what then?
Can you employ your leisure any better?
Give up your epigrams for tragedy
Or thunder brutal wars in epic verse
That pedants may recite you to their students
Who, when grown up, will hate you thoroughly?
No, let such verse be written by the poets,
Bookish and grave, who write by smoky lamps.
Keep giving Romans your books, laced with salt:
You know their nature and their manners, too.
Let someone think you're playing but a reed;
We'll still be hearing it when trumpets have died out."

VIII.12

Vxorem quare locupletem ducere nolim
    quaeritis? Vxori nubere nolo meae.
Inferior matrona suo sit, Prisce, marito:
    non aliter fiunt femina uirque pares.

VIII.19

Pauper uideri Cinna uult; et est pauper.

VIII.20

Cum facias uersus nulla non luce ducenos,
Vare, nihil recitas. Non sapis, atque sapis.

VIII.27

Munera qui tibi dat locupleti, Gaure, senique,
    si sapis et sentis, hoc tibi ait "Morere."

VIII.31

Nescio quid de te non belle, Dento, fateris,
    coniuge qui ducta iura paterna petis.
Sed iam supplicibus dominum lassare libellis
    desine et in patriam serus ab urbe redi:
nam dum tu longe deserta uxore diuque
    tres quaeris natos, quattuor inuenies.

VIII.12

Why won't I marry a rich woman? See:
I won't be taken to husband by a wife.
The wife should be subordinate for life.
Priscus, that's spousal true equality.

VIII.19

Cinna seems poor—and is, therefore.

VIII.20

Though Varus daily sits and writes—
Two hundred lines!—he neither tries
To publish verses nor recites.
He's not too witty, but he's wise.

VIII.27

Lavishing presents on your rich, gray head,
What is he saying, Gaurus, but "drop dead"?

VIII.31

You self-confess, Dento, when having married
You ask the rights of the father of three children.
Quit pestering Domitian and be stilled when
You finally return from fruitless, harried
Attempts to find three children outside Rome.
Behold! You'll find your wife with four at home.

VIII.53

Formosissima quae fuere uel sunt,
    sed uilissima quae fuere uel sunt,
o quam te fieri, Catulla, uellem
    formosam minus aut magis pudicam!

VIII.69

Miraris ueteres, Vacerra, solos
nec laudas nisi mortuos poetas.
Ignoscas petimus, Vacerra: tanti
non est, ut placeam tibi, perire.

VIII.76

"Dic uerum mihi, Marce, dic, amabo;
nil est quod magis audiam libenter."
Sic et cum recitas tuos libellos,
et causam quotiens agis clientis,
oras, Gallice, me rogasque semper.
Durum est me tibi quod petis negare.
Vero uerius ergo quid sit audi:
uerum, Gallice, non libenter audis.

VIII.53

You are a slut although with beauty graced.
Catulla, be less the stunner or more chaste.

VIII.69

Only the ancients stir your wonder;
You praise no poet but the dead, Vacerra.
Forgive me if I don't oblige. I'd rather
Not die just yet to win your small hosanna.

VIII.76

"Come, Marcus, tell me candidly:
Do you like it? Answer me."
So, pleading cases, you invite
My viewpoint; and when you recite,
Gallicus, still you ask and pray.
I know it's rude that I delay,
But listen, here's the truth, I swear it:
Gallicus, you don't want to hear it.

Book IX

IX.6

Dicere de Libycis reduci tibi gentibus, Afer,
continuis volui quinque diebus Have:
'Non vacat' aut 'dormit' dictum est bis terque reverso.
Iam satis est: non vis, Afer, havere: vale.

IX.5

Nubere vis Prisco: non miror, Paula; sapisti.
    Ducere te non vult Priscus: et ille sapit.

IX.10

Cenes, Canthare, cum foris libenter,
damas et maledicis et minaris.
deponas animos truces monemus:
liber non potes et gulosus esse.

IX.15

Inscripsit tumulis septem scelerata virorum
    'Se fecisse' Chloe. Quid pote simplicius?

IX.19

Laudas balnea versibus trecentis
cenantis bene Pontici, Sabelle.
vis cenare, Sabelle, non lavari.

IX.6

You're back from Africa now for five days.
When I come calling "sorry, he's asleep"
Or else "he's busy," so your servant says.
I've called three times. I'll let my greetings keep.
I've had enough. Don't want me to say hi?
That's fine, Afer, so I'll just say good-bye.

IX.5

Paula wishes to marry Priscus. Paula's wise.
So's Priscus; his rejection's no surprise.

IX.10

You dine at people's houses willingly,
Cantharus, but you rant and bitch and preach.
Listen: you can't have both; you must decide
If you prefer free dinners or free speech.

IX.15

Seven husbands' tombs read, carved in stone,
Chloe wrought this. What's more plainly known?

IX.19

Praising the great man's baths in fine,
Well-polished verse, line after line,
Sabellus would not bathe but dine.

IX.45

Miles Hyperboreos modo, Marcelline, triones
et Getici tuleras sidera pigra poli:
ecce Promethei rupes et fabula montis
quam prope sunt oculis nunc adeunda tuis!
videris inmensis cum conclamata querelis
saxa senis, dices 'Durior ipse fuit.'
et licet haec addas: 'Potuit qui talia ferre,
humanum merito finxerat ille genus.'

IX.50

Ingenium mihi, Gaure, probas sic esse pusillum,
carmina quod faciam quae brevitate placent.
Confiteor. Sed tu bis senis grandia libris
qui scribis Priami proelia, magnus homo es?
Nos facimus Bruti puerum, nos Langona vivum:
tu magnus luteum, Gaure, Giganta facis.

IX.52

Si credis mihi, Quinte, quod mereris,
natalis, Ovidi, tuas Aprilis
ut nostras amo Martias Kalendas.
felix utraque lux diesque nobis
signandi melioribus lapillis!
hic vitam tribuit sed hic amicum.
plus dant, Quinte, mihi tuae Kalendae.

IX.45

Marcellinus, when you set forth
To soldier in the frigid North
Beneath the Getic constellations,
Think how close those duty stations
Approach the famed Promethean rock
And fabled mountains! Taking stock
Of these—the hero's confidants
Who heard his cries—you'll say at once,
"Prometheus was harder!" Add:
"Who had—and without going mad—
Endured such suffering was fit
To mold clay, fashion men from it."

IX.50

Gaurus, though you pretend my talent's small
Because I write brief poems, let me say,
Sure, you're a great man writing twelve book epics,
But I limn life; you fashion men of clay.

IX.52

I love the first of April, your birthday,
Quintus Ovidius, as much as mine
On the first March. Two happy days! and may
Both days be marked with whitest stones aligned.
One gave me life and one a friend. I've known
Yours, Quintus, gave me much more than my own.

IX.74

Effigiem tantum pueri pictura Camoni
    servat et infantis parva figura manet.
florentes nulla signavit imagine voltus,
    dum timet ora pius muta videre pater.

IX.81

Lector et auditor nostros probat, Aule, libellos,
sed quidam exactos esse poeta negat.
non nimium curo: nam cenae fercula nostrae
malim convivis quam placuisse cocis.

IX.74

This portrait of the child Camonus holds for us
All we possess of that sweet infant, though it's dated.
His father keeps no likenesses of the young man,
Dreading to see his son no longer animated.

IX.81

Readers and listeners praise my books;
Some critic swears they're worse than a beginner's.
Aulus, who cares? I always plan my dinners
To please the diners, not the cooks.

Book X

X.1

Si nimius videor seraque coronide longus
    Esse liber, legito pauca: libellus ero.
Terque quaterque mihi finitur carmine parvo
    Pagina: fac tibi me quam cupis ipse brevem.

X.2

Festinata prior, decimi mihi cura libelli
    Elapsum manibus nunc revocavit opus.
Nota leges quaedam, sed lima rasa recenti;
    Pars nova maior erit: lector, utrique fave,
Lector, opes nostrae: quem cum mihi Roma dedisset.
    'Nil tibi quod demus maius habemus' ait.
'Pigra per hunc fugies ingratae flumina Lethes
    Et meliore tui parte superstes eris.
Marmora Messallae findit caprificus, et audax
    Dimidios Crispi mulio ridet equos:
At chartis nec furta nocent et saecula prosunt,
    Solaque non norunt haec monumenta mori.'

X.1

I seem too long, my end too far away?
Read a few poems—I'll be a little book.
Each page has three or four, and so you may
Abridge it and read where you want to look.

X.2

The work I gave my tenth book was so rushed
That I decided it required revision.
You'll see some epigrams you've seen before,
Now polished, but new work predominates.
Reader, like all of them. You're my support;
Rome granted you to me with solemn words:
"I've nothing greater to bestow on you;
They'll save you from the sluggish waves of Lethe,
Allow your better part's survival after
Messale's marble tomb succumbs to fig trees,
After the bawdy muleteer sneers at Crispus,
His statue with the mutilated chargers.
Poems are indestructible by time:
Such monuments alone preserve your name."

X.4

Qui legis Oedipoden caligantemque Thyesten,
Colchidas et Scyllas, quid nisi monstra legis?
Quid tibi raptus Hylas, quid Parthenopaeus et Attis,
Quid tibi dormitor proderit Endymion?
Exutusve puer pinnis labentibus? aut qui
Odit amatrices Hermaphroditus aquas?
Quid te vana iuvant miserae ludibria chartae?
Hoc lege, quod possit dicere vita 'Meum est.'
Non hic Centauros, non Gorgonas Harpyiasque
Invenies: hominem pagina nostra sapit.
Sed non vis, Mamurra, tuos cognoscere mores
Nec te scire: legas Aetia Callimachi.

X.8

Nubere Paula cupit nobis, ego ducere Paulam
    Nolo: anus est. Vellem, si magis esset anus.

X.13

Ducit ad auriferas quod me Salo Celtiber oras,
    pendula quod patriae uisere tecta iuuat,
tu mihi simplicibus, Materne, lectis,
    fac ueniat longa iam mihi tarda mora:
rura meae referam, Materne, relicta,
    et reminiscar ager noster ut ipse sonet.

X.4

You read of Oedipus and of Thyestes,
Medea and the Scyllas: fantasies!
Just what knowledge has the tale of Hylas,
Or of Parthenopaeus, or of Atys,
Or of that sleeping boy, Endymion,
Or wax-winged Icarus, or Hermaphroditus,
Given you? Lay aside frivolity
And read my books of poems for real life.
You'll find no Centaurs, Gorgons, Harpies there.
I write of man; but if, Mamurra, you
Have no desire to study men and manners,
Have no desire to know yourself, why then,
Sure, read the myths of old Callimachus.

X.8

Old Paula wants to marry me;
I give her the cold shoulder.
But I could take her seriously
If she were even older.

X.13

The River Salo draws me back to Spain,
My native rocky land; the reason's plain:
Manius, best friend from my childhood days
And youth, esteemed and worthy of my praise.
With you, the Libyan desert in a tent
Or Scythian hovel would be time well spent.
If our regard's still mutual, our home,
No matter where, will be our very Rome.

X.21

Scribere te quae vix intellegat ipse Modestus
Et vix Claranus, quid rogo, Sexte, iuvat?
Non lectore tuis opus est, sed Apolline libris:
Iudice te maior Cinna Marone fuit.
Sic tua laudentur sane: mea carmina, Sexte,
Grammaticis placeant, ut sine grammaticis.

X.24

Natales mihi Martiae Kalendae,
Lux formosior omnibus Kalendis,
Qua mittunt mihi munus et puellae,
Quinquagensima liba septimamque
Vestris addimus hanc focis acerram.
His vos, si tamen expedit roganti,
Annos addite bis precor novenos,
Ut nondum nimia piger senecta,
Sed vitae tribus areis peractis
Lucos Elysiae petam puellae.
Post hunc Nestora nec diem rogabo.

X.26

Vare, Paraetonias Latia modo vite per urbes
    Nobilis et centum dux memorande viris,
At nunc Ausonio frustra promisse Quirino,
    Hospita Lagei litoris umbra iaces.
Spargere non licuit frigentia fletibus ora,
    Pinguia nec maestis addere tura rogis.
Sed datur aeterno victurum carmine nomen:
    Numquid et hoc, fallax Nile, negare potes?

X.21

Just why, Sextus, do you delight in writing
What even shrewdest critics barely grasp?
Your books need Phoebus, not a common reader.
You judge that Cinna outstripped even Vergil.
May your books garner equal praise! For me,
If my small books can please grammarians,
I'm pleased—assuming they likewise please readers
Who don't require grammarians to guide them.

X.24

Kalends of March! My birthday! Day more happy
Than any other, on which maids send presents,
I set upon my hearth these cakes, this censer,
Celebrating fifty-seven years.
Add to them (if they're good) I beg of you
Just eighteen more so that I might descend
To the dark woods of the Elysian queen
While still unhobbled by the nagging years,
Achieving the third stage of life like Nestor.
Then I won't ask another single day.

X.26

O Varus, lately a centurion,
You lie now on a strange Egyptian shore.
Quirinus vainly waits you, but you're gone.
We can't place incense on your pyre nor pour
Our tears on your cracked lips. Immortal verse
Shall be our tribute. Nile, will you do worse?

X.29

Quam mihi mittebas Saturni tempore lancem,
    misisti dominae, Sextiliane, tuae;
et quam donabas dictis a Marte Kalendis,
    de nostra prasina est synthesis empta toga.
Iam constare tibi gratis coepere puellae:
    muneribus futuis, Sextiliane, meis.

X.40

Semper cum mihi diceretur esse
Secreto mea Polla cum cinaedo,
Inrupi, Lupe. Non erat cinaedus.

X.43

Septima iam, Phileros, tibi conditur uxor in agro.
    Plus nulli, Phileros, quam tibi, reddit ager.

X.47

Vitam quae faciant beatiorem,
Iucundissime Martialis, haec sunt:
Res non parta labore, sed relicta;
Non ingratus ager, focus perennis;
Lis numquam, toga rara, mens quieta;
Vires ingenuae, salubre corpus;
Prudens simplicitas, pares amici;
Convictus facilis, sine arte mensa;
Nox non ebria, sed soluta curis;
Non tristis torus, et tamen pudicus;
Somnus, qui faciat breves tenebras:
Quod sis, esse velis nihilque malis;
Summum nec metuas diem nec optes.

X.29
Sextilianus, that dish you used to gift me
On Saturnalia you've given to your mistress;
The cash that bought my birthday toga pays to dress
Your lady in a new green robe. How thrifty:
Your lovers cost you nothing—much to my distress.

X.40
The current rumor would indict
My Polla and a sodomite.
I caught them. Rumor wasn't right.

X.43
Phil's seventh wife lies buried in his field.
No other land returns so rich a yield.

X.47
The things which make a life of ease,
Martial, my dearest friend, are these:
The patrimony's easy yield;
A thriving fire and fertile field;
Neither the courts nor formal dress;
Good health; a wise judiciousness;
Some friends whose conversation's able
To dignify your simple table;
A wife with neither forwardness
Nor prudery; deep sleep to press
Over the shadows in swift flight;
Ability to see you're right
When you're content; and, with head clear,
Face death without desire or fear.

X.53

Ille ego sum Scorpus, clamosi gloria Circi,
    Plausus, Roma, tui deliciaeque breves,
Invida quem Lachesis raptum trieteride nona,
    Dum numerat palmas, credidit esse senem.

X.74

Iam parce lasso, Roma, gratulatori,
Lasso clienti. Quamdiu salutator
Anteambulones et togatulos inter
Centum merebor plumbeos die toto,
Cum Scorpus una quindecim graves hora
Ferventis auri victor auferat saccos?
Non ego meorum praemium libellorum
— Quid enim merentur? — Apulos velim campos:
Non Hybla, non me spicifer capit Nilus,
Nec quae paludes delicata Pomptinas
Ex arce clivi spectat uva Setini.
Quid concupiscam quaeris ergo? dormire.

X.53

I'm Scorpus, Rome, greatest of charioteers,
The short-lived champion, object of your cheers,
At twenty-seven, dead. Lachesis erred:
Counting my victories, she thought them years.

X.74

At length, O Rome, pity this weary client,
This bone-tired caller. Must I be reliant,
Among these hangers-on, on wasting days
Sweating for leaden tokens at this pace
While Scorpus drives an hour-long chariot race,
Lugging off fifteen sacks of gorgeous gold?
For my poor books, I would not wax so bold
To wish Apulian plains; neither the Nile,
Grain-laden, nor Mt. Hybla's charms beguile;
Nor tender Setine grapes, whose vines men keep
On hills above where Pomptine marshes seep.
You ask me, therefore, what I want? Some sleep.

X.75

Milia viginti quondam me Galla poposcit
    Et, fateor, magno non erat illa nimis.
Annus abit: 'Bis quina dabis sestertia' dixit.
    Poscere plus visa est quam prius illa mihi.
Iam duo poscenti post sextum milia mensem
    Mille dabam nummos. Noluit accipere.
Transierant binae forsan trinaeve Kalendae,
    Aureolos ultro quattuor ipsa petit.
Non dedimus. Centum iussit me mittere nummos:
    Sed visa est nobis haec quoque summa gravis.
Sportula nos iunxit quadrantibus arida centum;
    Hanc voluit: puero diximus esse datam.
Inferius numquid potuit descendere? fecit.
    Dat gratis, ultro dat mihi Galla: nego.

X.82

Si quid nostra tuis adicit vexatio rebus,
    mane vel a media nocte togatus ero
stridentesque feram flatus aquilonis iniqui
    et patiar nimbos excipiamque nives.
Sed si non fias quadrante beatior uno
    per gemitus nostros ingenuasque cruces,
parce, precor, fesso vanosque remitte labores,
    qui tibi non prosunt et mihi, Galle, nocent.

X.75

Once she demanded twenty thou, and I
Thought Galla cheaply priced. A year passed by:
"Will you give ten?" which strangely seemed still more
Than that full twenty she had cost before.
In six months it was two. Less than enthused,
I offered one. She haughtily refused.
Some two or three months later, she, resigned,
Asked for four gold coins and, when I declined,
Said something about discounts. I departed.
Next, my cheap dole had bought her—or she started
To say it had. I gave it to my slave.
Could she sink lower, if not in the grave?
O yes. In fact, she gives herself away,
But even that's too steep a price to pay.

X.82

Believe me, Gallus, just for you
I'll wear my toga and slog through
An early morning or midnight
If somehow my exertions might
Benefit you; and I'll endure
North winds, rain storms, and even more,
A deep snowfall; but if you've not
Improved a fraction of your lot,
Please cut your weary client loose,
Excuse him when he's of no use.
There's no advantage I can see,
Gallus, in pointless pain for me.

X.102

Qua factus ratione sit requiris,
    Qui numquam futuit, pater Philinus?
Gaditanus, Avite, dicat istud,
    Qui scribit nihil et tamen poeta est.

X.102

You want to know just how Philenus became
A father doing naught to claim that name?
Ask Gaditanus, devoted to the Nine,
Self-proclaimed bard who never wrote a line.

Book XI

XI.3

Non urbana mea tantum Pimpleide gaudent
otia, nec vacuis auribus ista damus
sed meus in Geticis ad Martia signa pruinis
a rigido teritur centurione liber,
dicitur et nostros cantare Britannia versus.
quid prodest? Nescit sacculus ista meus.
at quam victuras poteramus pangere chartas
quantaque Pieria proelia flare tuba,
cum pia reddiderint Augustum numina terris,
et Maecenatem si tibi, Roma, darent!

XI.14

Heredes, nolite brevem sepelire colonum:
    nam terra est illi quantulacumque gravis.

XI.24

Dum te prosequor et domum reduco,
aurem dum tibi praesto garrienti,
et quidquid loqueris facisque laudo,
quot versus poterant, Labulle, nasci!
Hoc damnum tibi non videtur esse,
si quod Roma legit, requirit hospes,
non deridet eques, tenet senator,
laudat causidicus, poeta carpit,
propter te perit? Hoc, Labulle, verum'st?
Hoc quisquam ferat? Ut tibi tuorum
sit maior numerus togatulorum,
librorum mihi sit minor meorum?
Triginta prope iam diebus una est
nobis pagina vix peracta. Sic fit
cum cenare domi poeta non vult.

XI.3

Not only city idlers love my Muse;
Nor do I write my verse for jaded ears;
But on the frosty Getian frontiers,
By battle standards, my epigrams amuse
The tough centurion; in Britain, too.
I'm famous, but my purse remains threadbare.
But what deep, epic trumpets could I dare,
And what immortal poems carry through,
Seeing the gods returned Augustus home,
If they'd restore Maecenas, too, O Rome.

XI.14

Oh heirs, don't bury this dwarf farmer; can't you see
Any amount of earth would lie too heavily?

XI.24

Labullus, while I'm trailing you through Rome
Or find myself escorting you back home,
Listening to your chatter, think of me
And think of my unwritten poetry.
You think it's nothing, what Rome reads,
Foreigner seeks, knight wants, senator needs,
Lawyer praises, and rival poets abuse
Are lost because of you? Is this fair use?
You add new clients, my books are diminished.
This past month, give or take, I've barely finished
A single poem, Labullus. It's the syndrome
Of poets who don't dine alone at home.

XI.35

Ignotos mihi cum voces trecentos,
quare non veniam vocatus ad te
miraris quererisque litigasque.
Solus ceno, Fabulle, non libenter.

XI.62

Lesbia se jurat gratis numquam esse fututam.
    Verum'st. Cum futui vult, numerare solet.

XI.66

Et delator es et calumniator,
et fraudator es et negotiator,
et fellator es et lanista. Miror
quare non habeas, Vacerra, nummos.

XI.79

Ad primum decima lapidem quod venimus hora,
arguimur lentae crimine pigritiae.
Non est ista viae, non est mea, sed tua culpa est,
misisti mulas qui mihi, Paete, tuas.

XI.93

Pierios vatis Theodori flamma penates
abstulit. Hoc Musis et tibi, Phoebe, placet?
O scelus, o magnum facinus crimenque deorum,
non arsit pariter quod domus et dominus!

XI.35

You have three hundred guests that I don't know,
Fabullus, then you grumble, bitch, and moan
When I return your dinner invitation.
Truth told, I've never liked to dine alone.

XI.62

Lesbia swears she's never a free lay.
That's true, because she always has to pay.

XI.66

Vacerra, you're a liar, informer, forger, spy;
And yet you're poor. I can't help wondering why.

XI.79

Nine hours it took to reach the first milestone,
And then you blame me like I broke some rules
By dawdling on my way. The fault's your own,
Paetus, for sending me decrepit mules.

XI.93

The flames destroyed this poet's house.
Muses, Apollo, say was this well done?
The very gods must find it scandalous
That house and Theo were not burned as one.

XI.97

Una nocte quater possum: sed quattuor annis
    si possum, peream, te Telesilla semel.

XI.99

De cathedra quotiens surgis—jam saepe notavi—,
pedicant miserae, Lesbia, te tunicae.
Quas cum conata es dextra, conata sinistra
vellere, cum lacrimis eximis et gemitu:
sic constringuntur gemina Symplegade culi
et nimias intrant Cyaneasque natis.
Emendare cupis vitium deforme? docebo:
Lesbia, nec surgas censeo nec sedeas.

XI.107

Explicitum nobis usque ad sua cornua librum
et quasi perlectum, Septiciane, refers.
Omnia legisti. Credo, scio, gaudeo, verum'st.
Perlegi libros sic ego quinque tuos.

XI.108

Quamvis tam longo possis satur esse libello,
lector, adhuc a me disticha pauca petis.
Sed Lupus usuram puerique diaria poscunt.
Lector, solve. Taces dissimulasque? Vale.

XI.97

I can cavort all night with four young dears.
You, Telesilla? Not once in four full years.

XI.99

When you stand, Lesbia, I see your gown
Treat you indecently, flat let you down.
You pluck it with your left hand then your right—
You're positively groaning!—it's held tight
In the Cyanean straits of your huge butt.
What's my advice? Don't stand. Don't sit. That's what.

XI.107

Septicianus, you return my book
Unrolled down to the end, as if read through.
You've read it; I believe and know it. Look,
Just so through all five books I've read you too.

XI.108

Such a long book should more than satisfy.
I've nothing more to add. You ask me why.
My creditors want cash; my slaves must eat.
Pay me for more. You're silent? Then good-bye.

Book XII

XII.10

Habet Africanus miliens, tamen captat.
   Fortuna multis dat nimis, satis nulli.

XII.12

Omnia promittis, cum tota nocte bibisti;
   Mane nihil praestas. Pollio, mane bibe.

XII.21

Municipem rigidi quis te, Marcella, Salonis
Et genitam nostris quis putet esse locis?
Tam rarum, tam dulce sapis. Palatia dicent,
Audierint si te vel semel, esse suam;
Nulla nec in media certabit nata Subura
Nec Capitolini collis alumna tibi;
Nec cito ridebit peregrini gloria partus,
Romanam deceat quam magis esse nurum.
Tu desiderium dominae mihi mitius urbis
Esse iubes: Romam tu mihi sola facis.

XII.25

Cum rogo te nummos sine pignore, 'non habeo' inquis;
   Idem, si pro me spondet agellus, habes:
Quod mihi non credis veteri, Telesine, sodali,
   Credis coliculis arboribusque meis.
Ecce, reum Carus te detulit: adsit agellus.
   Exilii comitem quaeris: agellus eat.

XII.10

With millions, Africanus still hunts legacies.
Some men have too much, none enough to please.

XII.12

All night you promise everything while drinking,
But come the next day, nil. Here's what we're thinking,
Pollio: next time you think to tie one on,
Hold off your guzzling till at least the dawn.

XII.21

Marcella, who would guess that you live here
Right on the banks of the iron-tempering Salo?
So sweet a character! The Princep's court,
Once hearing you, would claim you for its own.
No woman born in the Subura nor
The Capitoline Hill equals you, my lady.
No foreigner's more fit to be Rome's daughter.
You ease my yearning for the Queen of Cities
Because, Marcella, you're a Rome to me.

XII.25

I asked a loan without a guarantee:
"Dear Martial, I'm flat broke." So much for me.
Well, Telesinus, you've the cash to lend
My pledged farm but refuse your oldest friend
Credit extended cabbages and trees.
When Carus the informant's trickeries
Ensnare you, though, it's "Martial, lend an arm,
Ease this exile's condition." Ask my farm.

XII.56

Aegrotas uno decies aut saepius anno,
    Nec tibi, sed nobis hoc, Polycharme, nocet:
Nam quotiens surgis, soteria poscis amicos.
    Sit pudor: aegrota iam, Polycharme, semel.

XII.58

Ancillariolum tua te vocat uxor, et ipsa
    Lecticariola est: estis, Alauda, pares.

XII.65

Formosa Phyllis nocte cum mihi tota
Se praestitisset omnibus modis largam,
Et cogitarem mane quod darem munus,
Utrumne Cosmi, Nicerotis an libram,
An Baeticarum pondus acre lanarum,
An de moneta Caesaris decem flavos:
Amplexa collum basioque tam longo
Blandita, quam sunt nuptiae columbarum,
Rogare coepit Phyllis amphoram vini.

XII.68

Matutine cliens, urbis mihi causa relictae,
Atria, si sapias, ambitiosa colas.
Non sum ego causidicus, nec amaris litibus aptus,
Sed piger et senior Pieridumque comes;
Otia me somnusque iuvant, quae magna negavit
Roma mihi: redeo, si vigilatur et hic.

XII.56

You're ill ten times a year; it's hard on us;
And when you're healed and feeling in your prime,
You want your friends' congratulatory presents.
Polycharmus, fall ill one final time.

XII.58

Alauda courts a slave, his wife a litter-bearer.
I can't imagine any marriage fairer.

XII.65

A night of pleasure: Phyllis gave her all
In every way, and with the morning light
I pondered presents for that luscious doll.
A pound of Cosmus' perfumes seemed right,
Or maybe a fine piece of Spanish wool,
Or even ten gold coins; and then she threw
Her arms around me, kissed me, played the fool,
And, for a present, said a jug of wine would do.

XII.68

Morning clients, cause of my leaving Rome,
Be wise and cultivate our great men's halls.
I'm an old, weary poet come back home,
Not a slick lawyer greased for courtroom brawls.
Leisure and sleep entice me. What good's Spain:
I'm back in Rome if sleepless once again.

XII.79

Donavi tibi multa, quae rogasti;
    Donavi tibi plura, quam rogasti:
Non cessas tamen usque me rogare.
    Quisquis nil negat, Atticilla, fellat.

XII.92

Saepe rogare soles, qualis sim, Prisce, futurus,
    Si fiam locuples simque repente potens.
Quemquam posse putas mores narrare futuros?
    Dic mihi, si fias tu leo, qualis eris?

XII.95

Musseti pathicissimos libellos,
    qui certant Sybariticis libellis,
et tinctas sale pruriente chartas
    Instanti lege, Rufe; sed puella
sit tecum tua, ne talassionem
    indicas manibus libidinosis
et fias sine femina maritus.

XII.79

I gave you what you asked, more than you asked;
And yet you keep on asking. As I live,
Atticilla, I've got to say one tasked
With constant giving soon has naught to give.

XII.92

Priscus, what sort of person would I be
If rich and powerful suddenly?
Priscus, if you turned lion suddenly,
What sort of lion would you be?

XII.95

Istantius Rufus, read the pathic books
Of Mussetius, like those Sybaris wrote
With their lascivious wit, but you take care
To have your lady with you lest you make
Your lusty hands sing out your wedding song,
And you become a husband with no wife.

Closing Poem

Martial in Bilbilis to Juvenal in Rome

Know what, dear Juvenal? While you are slogging
Across the racket of Subura or dogging
Diana's hill, jostled by pimps and whores,
Catamites, muggers, thugs in darkened doors,
Property speculators, politicians
And lawyers, Romans without inhibitions—
All those types who activate your spleen—
Your good friend Martial's nowhere to be seen.
My friend, stand in your toga drenched with sweat
(However much you flap it, it stays wet)
Waiting at thresholds of your high-powered friends.
I'm in Bilbilis, making my amends
For all the sleep lost. I'm a gentleman;
After the long years gone, my city can,
And does, take to her bosom her lost son.
I have no clients here nor anyone
Disturbing peaceful sleep, at least till nine!
I wear no toga, any old clothes of mine
Suffice when I awake. There's a fire burning
In the hearth, laid by my steward, and my yearning
For a good breakfast's quickly satisfied
By his wife's breakfast, almost countrified.
A little later comes my housemaid, who'd
Have you, friend, drooling to end her maidenhood
As she cleans up the bowls and sweeps the floors.
My young attendants start their daily chores.
Thus home, city of iron and gorgeous gold!
(You know, if you will let me be so bold,
I'd say that epithet describes my epigrams.)
I hear you snarling a long string of damns!
I'm sorry, Juvenal, but this is why
Delight crowns all my days, and here I'll die.